The Poetry of

Janie Luelling Byrnes

The Poetry of Janie Luelling Byrnes
First Edition

Published by Byrnes, Finger and Hoffman
Canby, Oregon

Edited and Designed by
Pamela Byrnes, Peggy Byrnes, Terrence Byrnes,
Terry Byrnes, and Genevieve Hoffman

Illustrations by
John Finger

Library of Congress Catalog Number 89-81879
ISBN 0-9625195-0-2

Printed in the United States of America

Preface

The poems presented in this publication were selected after great deliberation. Janie Luelling Byrnes was a prolific writer and produced many more poems than could be included in this volume. Works were selected to exemplify the range of her poetry and to illustrate her life, wisdom, and the times in which she lived. "Heritage" reveals how she felt about her ancestry, "The Mountains From a Moving Train" gives us some insight into her innermost feelings about herself, and "Old?" poignantly expresses her response to aging. Some poems were included because they have been family favorites for several generations and others because they hold special meaning for her friends, family or community. Her poetry is presented as she wrote it, retaining the word spelling and usage of her time. Dates are included whenever possible.

This book is dedicated to anyone who can use a word of inspiration, solace for a lost loved one, guidance in times of trouble, or simply a word of cheer.

Janie Ellen Luelling Byrnes, Age 95, Spring 1988

Author's Note [*]

Perhaps I should explain this book. These are not all finished rhymes, but oft are thoughts — a changing view — in which one thread of thought runs true; and that is LOVE . . . love for home and family, and country, nature, mankind too — God's children all — the lovable and the lost, and most of all a deep and trusting love for my dear Lord.

— Janie Luelling Byrnes

* Taken from JLB's 1979 handwritten book of poems

About the Author

Janie Ellen Luelling Byrnes
1892 - 1988

Janie Luelling Byrnes was a poet both with words
and in the way she lived her life. She was a true
naturalist, lover of the world's beauty, a daily
conserver of our planet's resources, and a kind,
religious woman who fed the homeless long before
such social issues had gained wide-spread public
notice. She loved the majestic mountains of her
beloved Oregon, visiting with the neighborhood
children, and her garden with all its fruit trees,
flowers and memories. She was an avid reader,
well versed in the works of great poets and writers.
Janie was delighted by the words of Will Rogers
and found answers in the Bible to calm her soul.
Above all, her faith and love of God carried her
through some hard and trying times during her
95 years.

She was born December 3, 1892 in Canby, Oregon.
Soon after, her family moved to a homestead near
Prineville, Oregon where she and her four younger
siblings were raised. Her Aunt Janie Harriet
Luelling, a well-educated woman and an accom-
plished writer and poet, inspired her to begin
writing poetry at a young age. Janie was proud of
her family heritage. Her ancestors, the Luelling
and Campbell families, had settled in Oregon and
earned historical importance as community leaders,
nurserymen and educators. This heritage,
combined with her experiences as a child in the
pioneer west, greatly influenced her poetry.

In the early 1900's, Janie worked in a variety of jobs. In Portland, she worked for the telephone company as an operator. She then moved to San Francisco, California where she worked in an import tea shop, a sewing shop, and a candy factory. In 1924 she moved to Tracy, California. There Janie served as president of the Tracy Women's Club, promoted the high school poetry club, and was very active in the church and the PTA. She was a recognized poet under the pen name of Jane L. Byrnes and attended the Annual Poet's Dinners in Oakland. At the age of 62, after her two children were grown and married, Janie returned to Canby with her husband, Terrence E. Byrnes, to care for her aging father.

In Canby, Janie devoted much of her community efforts to the United Methodist Church and the needs of the elderly. She visited residents of local nursing homes to offer help and friendship until she was in her nineties. She taught Sunday School and was looked upon as a wise elder of her church. She volunteered her time to serve meals at "Loaves and Fishes" and mailed church bulletins to shut-ins.

Her concern and understanding for the elderly never excluded her love and interest in the young. She studied her rapidly changing world through books, movies, music, technology, and the emerging customs and issues to understand what young people faced. She met the modern world with an open mind and heart, offering love and understanding to people of all ages. Up until the time of her death in June, 1988, she remained active at church, wrote poetry and cared for her garden.

Janie Ellen Luelling Byrnes, Age 19, 1911

Heritage

The West is mine.
It is my Heritage.
Its peace, its promise, its prosperity,
Its rugged inspiration and its truth,
Its songs, its legends, and its solitudes.

I am the child
Of Pioneers.

Those dreaming, rugged
Sons of Toil
Who loved their God in spirit — yet

Disdaining not the soil
Did well the task they set themselves to do.
They saw in dreams
What we in fact may see:
Vast fields of grain and orchard plots,
And cities thriving by the sea.

For this they lay the cornerstone
And marked the pattern of the walls;
And that far greater cornerstone
The future ages yet unborn,
And marked the pattern
Of their souls.

I am of these.

And this is mine.
I dedicate my dream to them.

Man's proper monument is man!
And I shall carve my soul to fit
The pattern of their mighty Plan
And stamp it on my children's soul
As it was stamped on mine.
Thus shall to consummation grow
The thing they dreamed so long ago,
And thus shall I account to them
And justify my Heritage!

Contents

The World Awakes

A Gift of Time

Dauntless Spirit

The World Awakes

The World Awakes

I awoke, looked from my window,
   Saw the day had just begun.
Like fairy worlds the tiny dew-drops
   Sparkled in the morning sun.

I saw a tardy owl returning,
   Silent as he flit along,
Heard a robin greet the morning
   With an ecstasy of song.

I saw the morning glories stirring
   Ere they opened their sleepy eyes,
Saw a sunbeam stoop to kiss them,
   Saw them wake in mock surprise.

I heard the meadowlark a-calling
   In the grasses o'er the way,
Saw the world in all its beauty
   Wake to greet the new-born day.

Woodland Pathway

Once I roamed the woods at mid-day
  With a troubled heart and sore —
When I spied a hidden pathway
  I had never seen before.

It was such a lovely pathway
  Reaching in among the trees,
Every leaf an elfin finger
  Beckoned gently in the breeze.

Here and there an errant sunbeam —
  Golden dart from unseen hand —
Turned the leaves to gold and silver
  Like a scene from fairyland.

Kissed by flowers a tiny brooklet
  Murmuring as it sped along
Over mossy twig and pebble
  Waked the silence with its song.

'Neath my feet a magic carpet
  Lade the air with woodland scent,
High o'erhead the great trees sighing
  Like a heart that's found content.

There I paused amidst its beauty
  Old rebellions strangely stilled
As the purpose of the ages
  In that moment seemed fulfilled.

Now when doubts and fears o'ertake me
    And my heart with care is spent
Memory leads me down that pathway
    With its message of content.

1925

Song of Oregon

Impossible to paint with song
    The beauty that is Oregon.
No words could show for mortal eye
    The mountains etched against the sky
With snowcapped peaks and stately pines —
    The mossy dells with columbines —
The rhododendrons' sweet profusion
    Blending the scenes in wild confusion;
Majestic cliffs where water falls
    In white cascade through mountain walls
Then rushes on eternally
    To find the sea — to find the sea.

Valleys that spread their endless green
    Where orchards bloom in early spring,
Where wild birds wake to greet the days —
    Robins — and Meadowlarks — and Jays —
Where every leaf is drenched with dew,
    And Faith and Hope are born anew.
No words could ever paint in song
    The Beauty that is Oregon.

1978

In a Forest Glade

Dappled leaves a-glancing
    In the forest glade,
Merry waters twinkling
    In the sun and shade.
Tiny birdlets whisper
    In the leafy bower;
While bees beg for honey
    From each fragrant flower.
A breeze is softly sighing
    Like a lullaby,
To each woodland creature
    As it passes by.

Dainty little snowflakes
    By the breezes whirled
Spread a lovely blanket
    O'er the sleeping world;
Hushed the merry brooklet,
    Hushed the busy bees
All the flowers are hidden
    'Neath the shelt'ring trees
All the little birdies
    Long ago have flown
Following the sunshine
    To its winter home.

The God that sends the sunshine
    To make the flowers grow
Hides them from the winter
    Beneath a robe of snow,

Wraps the naked branches
    Of the leafless trees
In the richest ermine
    That they may not freeze;
And when the winter's over
    The brook will sing anew
With the happy birds and bees
    "Thanks, dear God, to you."

1928

The Cry of the Wind

The wind in the trees as it sobs and raves
    Sounds like the echo of ocean waves
As they dash themselves on the rocky shore
    And muttering, stunned, recede once more,
Broken and sobbing in sullen rage
    At the endless battle they must wage;
It breaks on the world with the weary blast
    That the waves on the rugged shore are cast.

The wind has the haunting sound of the sea
    With its fury, its mystery, its energy;
The whispering, menacing, silence and roar;
    The breaking and ebbing, o'er and o'er;
And the Demon of Havoc that rides in its path
    Is lashed on its way by the ocean's wrath.
Born of the caverns, sired by the sea;
    Is this why it echoes such savagery?

To an Old Tree

Ye gaunt and aged sentinel,
    Upon yon rocky mountain peak,
What is the message thou wouldst give
    The trees about thy aged feet?

Oh! Wouldst thou bid them seek the vale,
    Or scale the lofty peaks with thee,
The greater battle there to wage,
    The greater vision there to see?

When gentle winds disturbed the glen
    Ye wrestled with the mighty gale;
But often thou in sunshine stood
    While fog enwrapped the lowly vale.

And thou couldst look across the sea;
    The ships beheld thee, passing by;
From out thy branches, loud and bold
    The eagle screamed his warning cry.

Now, with thy naked arms upraised
    Art thou protesting at thy fate,
Or art thou giving thanks to God,
    Or pleading with thy death to wait?

The reason for this weary strife
    Hast thou yet found or still must seek?
Art thou a warning or dost beckon
    Unto the trees about thy feet?

Dost warn them that the fight is vain,
    Or bid them climb to know its worth
To where, in aged majesty,
    Ye stand, cloud-crowned, above the earth?

The Evergreens of Oregon

O Evergreens of Oregon,
O guardians of a mighty state,
Like dark-robed saints that age on age
'Twixt heaven and earth propitiate.

How often as a little child
I dreamed beneath your sun-flecked shade
Or roamed down stately avenues
Where ray of sunshine never strayed.

The weary years have left their scar
Upon the face of earth and man,
The child that dreamed beneath your shade
Now backward turns to dream again.

And still I feel your mystery
Where perfumed shadows deepest lie,
And still I love to hear you croon
Your sea-born song against the sky.

Unmindful of the sands of time
You watch serene against the sun
As symbols of Eternity,
O Evergreens of Oregon.

1930

There Is a Season

Suddenly there was Spring —
  And Beauty walking — shyly —
  Tip-toeing in and out among the hills
  And all the secret corners
  Where the young sun spills
  Its soft new warmth upon the heart . . .
  Where nature's breast
  Gathers for Beauty's minions
  All that is best.

Then quietly it was Summer —
  And Beauty walking — regally —
  Amid the flowers, full blossomed now
  And among them, the wealth of green;
  The green of trees —
  The shades of simple grasses
  And the sheen
  Of sunlight over all.
  Summer — pregnant with promise
  For the harvest's call.

Then there was Autumn —
  And Beauty walking — joyously —
  Maternal now — full bosomed —
  Wise to the purpose of the tender Spring
  Wise to the summer's pregnant seed,
  Aware of every fruit and every bloom,
  Seed-laden for the next spring's certain need.

And then came Winter —
  And Beauty walking with a slower step
  Her arms heavy with fertile seed —
  Promise of every growing thing —
  To find a place of rest — while winter ravaged —
  A sheltering cover for the precious seed,
  The life-germ of each growing thing.
  Then Beauty bowed her snow white head — to wait.

And suddenly — There was Spring!

1968

Saturnalia

On her gaily slippered feet
Autumn dances down the street;
Dances out upon the hill;
Dances down beside the rill;
Dances in the wooded glen,
Back across the field again;
On her gaily slippered feet
Dances back into the street.

Autumn lifts her tawny eyes
Mad with daring to the skies;
Lifts her ruffled flounces free,
Dips a curtsy tauntingly;
Shakes the red leaves from her hair,
Sends them whirling everywhere
As she lifts her tawny eyes

Drenched with passion from the skies.

Gone the purpose of the Spring,
Gone the time of blossoming,
Gone the bondage and the care
Of the Summer's sultry air;
Gone the seasons' awful need —
Like from like from soil to seed —
Gone the purpose of the Spring
With the time of harvesting.

Now she wheels in pagan mood
Through the byways and the wood,
Where the red-lipped gypsies wait,
With the West Wind for her mate.
While in Bacchanalian strain
Time beats out the swift refrain,
Pagan Autumn's perfumed breath
Pulses to the Dance of Death.

Song of the North Wind

I come from the caves of the frozen north
    At the edge of the ice-bound sea —
The frosty breath of the snow clad plain
    Is the breath of life to me.
Gaily I buffet the mountains of ice,
    Or dash with a roar of wrath
At some magic palace, crystal spired,
    That has drifted across my path.
Away to the forests I whirl with joy,
    With ice and snow and noise;

I seal up the rivers to silence their mirth,
    The giant trees are my toys.
Then over the waters of leaden blue
    I rush with a clap of glee
And toss them about 'til in fury unbound
    They seek to encapture me.
But I rush away to the world of men,
    There is much there I can do,
For I bear as my burden a bounteous pack
    Of good, and bad things too.
I can lade the earth with a blanket of snow
    That my breath may cause no pain,
And then in a spirit of reckless mirth
    I may whisk it off again.
I can paint the cheeks of the girls and boys
    'Til they blush like a summer's rose,
I can brighten their eyes and toss their curls
    Or else I may frost their nose.
I dash the lingering leaves to the earth
    I chase them everywhere
Then sift some snow o'er the naked trees
    That they may not seem so bare.
I gather new strength as I hurry along
    Louder, more boastful, am I
As I race at the night with fiendish glee
    And a savage, howling cry.
I visit the ships on the wild sea's breast
    And round them I scream and roar
'Til wearied, then gather my waning strength
    And go racing on once more —
But the lonely caves of my frozen north
    Are calling again to me,
My breath grows warm — I must hurry away —
    To the edge of the ice-bound sea.

California

They can paint you, California,
　　In the glorious, golden spring,
But they cannot paint your music
　　When contented wild birds sing;
Nor the tender silver glimmering
　　Of the dew on everything
When the sun comes gently smiling
　　In the early morn of spring.
They can paint your fairy orchards
　　'Gainst blue mountains capped with snow,
But they cannot paint their perfume
　　As the vagrant breezes blow;
Nor the secret of the promise
　　That their blossoms white bestow,
Nor the songs the bees are humming
　　As they gaily come and go.
They can paint the mighty monarchs
　　In your forests far and near,
But they cannot paint their soughing
　　In the springtime of the year;
Nor the trilling of the brooklets
　　That come flowing crystal clear
From your hoary-headed mountains
　　With their songs of life and cheer.
They can paint your fields all mottled,
　　Gay with flowers of every hue,
Fields aflame with golden poppies,
　　Buttercups, and lupines blue;
Paint your sunshine, paint your shadows,
　　Paint your hills and valleys too,
But they cannot, California,
　　Paint the love we have for you.

1930

Vacation Hunger

I am weary of the city,
    Its eternal round of care,
Its sidewalks' ceaseless echoes,
    And the walls that seem to stare
As they rise like the walls of a prison
    Shutting the world from view,
Except, like a well inverted,
    One glimpse of vaulted blue.

I am weary of my fellows
    That pass unheeding by
Their faces ever window-ward
    With blank or wistful eye.

I am hungry for the mountains,
    For the peace of hill and dale
Where the footfalls' gentle echoing
    Wakes whispers in the vale;
Where drowsy lakes lie dreaming
    In the sunset's afterglow,
Their mirrored depths revealing
    The mountains crowned with snow,
With tall pines boldly etching
    Their forms where shadows play,
And rugged peaks incarnadined
    With the blood of the dying day.

There I would sate my soul on peace
    Till it turned from the cloying sweet
And drove me back content to walk
    With the crowds in the city's street.

1928

San Francisco

The morning stirs as the sun's first beam
Pierces the fog with a shadowy gleam,
Charging the white mist merrily,
Driving it out — far out — to sea,
Leaving the captive city free.
       Sing ho, my heart, sing ho!

The sun leaps up from the distant hills,
The sapphire depth of the great bay thrills,
Ferries like shuttles weave out and in,
Sea gulls are screaming their hoarse-voiced din —
What a wonderful way for a day to begin.
       Sing ho, my heart, sing ho!

The long shades vanish, the sun rides high
In regal splendor across the sky,
And the busy crowds on their daily beat
Their hearts attuned to their eager feet,
Give smile for smile in the sun-drenched street.
       Sing ho, my heart, sing ho!

Softly a breeze wafts in from the sea —
What is the message it brings to me?
Bearing to me in its outstretched hand
A perfumed note from a foreign land;
I know today I shall understand.
       Sing ho, my heart, sing ho!

The shadows lengthen, the hour grows late,
The sun sinks low through the Golden Gate,
Flinging its streamers bright and gay
Over the city, the hills, the bay.
Veiling the end of a perfect day.
       Sing ho, my heart, sing ho!

1928

Evening

The Sky, still blushing from the Sun-god's
                    Good-night kiss
Upon her crimson lips, half breathless with
                    The moment's bliss,
Stoops o'er the lake, beholds her radiant
                    Likeness there.
The silent shadows, falling o'er her brow
                    Like dusky hair,
Quick veil the vision, dim the lake's
                    Bright gleam,
But still she lingers in the darkness there,
                    To dream.
Then comes the Moon, fair hand-maid
                    Of the night,
And gently wraps her in a robe of
                    Silver light,
And once again the mirrored vision
                    To behold,
Pins back the errant tresses with a thousand
                    Stars of gold.

Evening in the Willamette Valley

Purple and gold the distant mountains lie
Like piles of tossed down tapestry
Their folds in broken symmetry
Ruffling the bottom edges of the sky.

1977

Peace

Last night I sat on the
    point of a star
And dabbled my feet in the
    cool dark pool of space.
The unimaginable
    silence of infinity
Swirled like an invisible
    mist about my face . . .
Hushing the harsh cacophony
    of earthly sounds
With the magic wand of
    omnipotent grace.
Leaving no sound of war,
    or strife, or sin.
The silence folded my
    spirit in.

And in all that space
There was only God
    and me.

1977

The Humble Singer

If a bird sings out from the mountain top
    How many are there to know?
But many there are to hear the song
    That is sung in the vale below.

So humbly I sit in the vale and sing —
    And many an eye grows bright —
And know not envy of sweeter songs
    That are sung on the mountain's height.

For those who have scaled the mountain's top
    And can hear that golden voice
Know other beauties besides his song
    To make their hearts rejoice.

But those who dwell in the work-walled vale,
    Busy and full of care
May list as they toil to the voice of the bird
    That sings in the shadows there.

So humbly I sit in the vale and sing,
    And many a care grows light
In a heart that never
    would have heard the songs
That are sung on the
    mountain's height.

1950

Morning Song

This morning I woke up singing
With a strange new joy in my heart.

The sun was gently beaming
And seemed to be a part
Of the sudden sense of living —
A new and bright beginning —
What joy it does impart!

This morning I woke up singing;
What a way for a day to start.

1984

Fame

Misjudge not of the quality of Fame:
How few there are that ere have writ their name
On stone that can withstand the ages' wear
That built not first on faith in God and man,
That learned not first to love and understand,
That did not serve and so learn to forebear.

Seek not to write your name upon the sand:
But carve it with a patient, careful hand
And Love's own chisel ere your strength departs;
That when all else of earth shall pass away
And men stand judged upon that final day
Your right to Fame be written on their hearts.

Weaving

Take a silver thread of Thought,
    Take a golden Deed,
Take the rosy Smile it brought
    (Many smiles you'll need).
Take about a yard of Song,
    A Whistle if you find it,
Some Loyalty to help along
    And Love enough to bind it.
Take a soft-hued strand of Prayer,
    Take a kind Word spoken,
Take the rainbow strands so rare
    Of Friendship, true, unbroken,
Take some Sunshine and some Flowers,
    A bit of pleasant Play,
And weave a wondrous Robe of Hours
    And call it Everyday.

To Cheer One Up

A little bright, a little light
A little bit of mirth
Is better still for many an ill
Than all the pills on earth.
A lonely heart will often start
To leave its care awhile
When a word of cheer dries up a tear
And wakes a little smile.

1972

Do Your Part

Because you can't control the earth
    Is no sign you should sigh;
Because life does not always give
    The things you want, don't cry.
Because you have to think of others
    That you meet along the way,
Don't grumble; show a smiling face,
    In smiles you'll reap your pay.

Make the best of every chance you have
    To help the world along
And you'll find it's glad to have you;
    You'll be welcomed with a song.
This old world will seem quite pleasant
    With a generous, friendly heart
If you'll smile and make the best of things
    And strive to do your part.

Success

There is little enough accomplished,
    There is little enough to the scheme,
But, oh, the hope in the doing,
    And, oh, the joy in the dream.
'Tis not alone the achieving,
    Nor what is to be the pay,
But what have you done to be winning,
    And how have you marked the way.

1926

Introspection

What is this vague unrest?
    Is it unhappiness,
That e'en when things seem best
    I still must feel its stress?

Perhaps it is, in part,
    Some duty should be done,
Or maybe in my heart
    Some victory to be won.

Have I, on some past day,
    Done ought I should repent?
Or have I missed the way
    That would have brought content?

Perhaps it is an urge
    Some greater thing to do;
Perhaps 'tis genius' surge
    To fame and fortune woo.

Perhaps I do not take
    The blessings of today,
The 'things that are' forsake,
    To wish some other way.

Perhaps 'tis that my mind
    Knows not the things worthwhile —
Oh, well! some way I'll find
    To hide it with a smile.

"My Own United States"

Why all this heated argument
    Between the east and west,
This shaking fist 'neath hostile nose,
    About whose state is best?
Why, when we speak of other states —
    If criticize we must,
To make our own state seem the best,
    Can't we at least be just?

Now all this useless quarreling
    Should make us blush with shame,
We need not knock our neighbor's home,
    Our own worth to proclaim.
Why can't we join all hands around,
    Be done with petty hates?
Oh, let us sing, in glad accord,
    "My Own United States."

1928

Our Soldier Dead

1918 World War I

Come! You must go to battle
    This is the great Crusade
    Fought for the greatest Cause
Since Wars for Christ were made.

Come forth, O Flower of Youth,
    To war! Ye Pride of all the Land —

Make the World Safe for Democracy!
This is the great command.

This is the war to end all wars
    No more youth's crimson stain
    Shall be poured forth on battle fields
In wars of lust or gain.

1928

Dear God of Love — what a travesty
    Our bones are not yet dust
    Brothers still living bear their wounds
Our guns are not yet rust!

Dear God of Peace — what irony
    That war could end man's lust
    We hear the war drums beat again
Before our bones are dust.

We hear the tramp of countless feet,
    The grueling soldier tread
    Where secret armies drill for war
Above our unmarked bed.

New instruments of death are born
    New weapons come to birth
    More awesome than the ones we knew
To sweep again this earth.

1938

Oh, now again, the War God stirs
    To test his dormant power,
    Sporadic terror stalks and hides
Against the coming hour.

Untitled

Some souls there are that soar majestically
    Above the deeps of this tumultuous life
And some there are that struggle endlessly
    Against the eddying flow; and in its strife
Grow strong enough to win above the tide
    While others in the treacherous undertow
        Are swept aside
                — Into oblivion

Defiance

Ho! Life, you would seek to crush me,
    Well you can't. I'll find a way.
With prayers and labor, and service to others,
    My debt to you I'll pay.

Ho! Life, you would drive me backward,
    When I seek to go ahead,
Well today is mine. I shall build anew.
    The aching past is dead.

Ho! Life, you would try to discourage
    As you call the battle vain.
You can't, for my soul is going to win
    The right to live again.

Could This Be Prophecy?

In the beginning God decreed
    That man should toil
To wrest his living from the soil
    And this some do
While others sit in rich estate
And justify the toiler's fate
    By that decree.

Then one day, man
    Built a machine — to fit *his* plan
To do his work and give him time
    To live — and play.
But in his new found liberty
He did not see machines could be
    A menace to God's own decree.

Today machines
    Like legendary Frankensteins
    Usurp man's place in God's design
    To earn his living from the land.
    Now nuts and bolts and gears and wires,
    Belching smoke, and screaming tires —
        Secret listening devices —
        The 'one-armed bandit' that entices —
        Computers ruling every station,
        Gathering secrets of the nation —
        Behemoths roaring down our highways —
        Wrecking forests and the byways —
        One machine reaps harvests when
        It would give work to a hundred men —

The thousands now who walk the lands
    In search of toil for idle hands.
Computerize this — let ten men go
    Automate that — a hundred more —
One man can do the work of ten.
One man to punch a button then —
    That starts a motor
    That runs a belt
    That loads a van
And it will use just one lone man.

What will man do with idle time?
Where will he go to get his bread
That soul and body may be fed?
Welfare — his lot? What travesty
He will not fare well
On such a dole. Man was made
To earn his living by his toil . . .
    By God's decree.

Man thought to make machines to serve.
    He did not see how soon
His masters they would be
As like a tide they sweep him out
Relentlessly — from every side
A mindless and relentless tide.
Man must assert supremacy
Over all crass machinery
Win back the promise of the soil
Win back the dignity of toil
Rely upon God's great command.
    Man is the keeper of the land!
The keeper, yes — to love and use,

Protect, conserve but not abuse.
Oh man, if you procrastinate
You soon must cry: Too late — too late.

Awake, mankind, awake and see
The person you are meant to be
    By God's decree.

1975

The Dreamer

Alone he stands upon the narrow ledge
    His shattered dreams have builded for his soul
Gathering bits of odd philosophies
    To build a fence along the too-close shoal;
To substitute a deep abiding faith
    Clutching at fragments of religious creeds —
And swift ambitions that can never reach
    A goal to satisfy his brave heart's needs.

Bewildered at the world's swift passing by,
    With hands too gentle for the task, he sought
To mold his dreams into reality
    And saw their fragile beauty come to naught.
Still brave, he waits upon his narrow ledge
    Gathering his tattered dreams about his soul,
And gazing out into Eternity
    Dreams on — that Faith "up there"
        Will find its goal.

1965

The Inheritance

So long had this land lain fallow
    A stranger to spade and plow
With only the tares of the meadow
    To feed at its breast until now.
But mine is the hand that shall till it
    Shall turn it and sow it with care
And after a season of tending
    Shall harvest the crops it will bear.

The fences that once rimmed the meadow,
    The neat patterned rails in a line
Are lost in a tangle of verdure
    Of hazel-bush, fern-brake, and vine.
Defeated, the old house stands barren
    Worn bleak by the sun and the wind —
The blight of the winters fall heavy
    On a house that is cold from within.

The cattle are gone from the pastures,
    The stables are empty close by,
The pathway that leads to the wellhouse
    Is hidden by milkweed — man high.
Undaunted — I see it tomorrow
    When the work of reclaiming is done —
When bright silver lines march the fences —
    In the pastures the young cattle run.

And I and my wife stand together
    To watch past the children at play,
As my grandfather stood here with his wife
    And dreamed in his heart of today.

I know that my pleasure would please him,
    How right to his mind it would seem
That the son of his son should inherit
    Not only his land — but his dream.

1958

Compassion

Dreams — dreams — the whole world dreams —
    Easing its heart by the magic of dreams —
Dreams of the future; dreams of the past;
Dreams a success that is unsurpassed;
Dreams of its dreams of empires won;
Dreams of a rest — with labors done;
Comforts its loss by dreaming of gain,
And so finds ease in the hour of pain;
Dreams of accomplishing some great deed
As a recompense in the hour of need;
Dreams of the day when all great things
Will wait at its feet with folded wings —
    But O, to me it oft times seems,
It will break its heart with dreaming dreams.

Protection

When the heart is full of happiness
    Then worry and care must retire
Like two grey wolves of the wilderness
    Held at bay by the friendly fire.

The City

I

On little ghostly feet
   The fog creeps in
Tucking the city
   Under a blanket of poisons
All its own — the city weeps
   In its own
       Pollution.

1974

II

Sleepily the river moves on its way
   To the sea
Inexorably — Relentlessly — Eternally —
   Cutting the city into two;
Bridges like giant spider webs
   Clinging on shore and shore
Seem to be trying
   To hold the city
       Together.

1979

Softly the noise of the day
Fades into the hush of evening;
Swiftly the shadows creep
Out of the storeroom of the night.

The Grim Jester

In the court of Life there watches one,
　　A jester, gray and grim,
Who plays with those that gather 'bout
　　Like puppets on a string.

As grouped about the festive board
　　The wine of joy to quaff,
With horrid leer and mocking smile
　　The jester seems to laugh.

As one would gaily toast his loves
　　The flowing wine he sips,
The jester with mock-serious face
　　Will dash it from his lips.

And here is one that sought great wealth
　　At any price 'twas bought,
Who sacrificed the souls of men
　　To gain the goal he sought.

But just as he has gained his goal
　　The jester strikes him down
And jeering stands beside his cot,
　　A gibbering, taunting clown.

Here one whose toys are hearts of men,
　　Whose beauty is her pride,
The jester dons the mask of death
　　And dances at her side.

A father seeks to sell his child
    More luxury to know —
The ancient purchaser beheld —
    The jester bids him "Go!"

And as he hears his puppets groan
    The festive board about
He dances round in fiendish glee
    With taunting laugh and shout.

*   *   *   *   *

But there are hearts not at this board
    A better fate for them —
The jester is more kind to those
    Who love their fellowmen.

Patterns

What kind of a pattern
Are you drawing for living?

Will it be a pattern for getting,
Or a model for giving?

Is it a pattern to glorify pleasure,
Or a plan to make wholeness your treasure?

For the garment you make from your present endeavor
May be the one you will wear forever and ever.

1984

The Old-timer

It is a merry song he sings
  As he walks along the way,
For he never is bothered by what has been
  Or about some yesterday.

He sings of days when he rode the range,
  Or travelled a city street;
He sings of a time when the tempest raged,
  Or a time when love was sweet.

He sings of a time his youth-days knew —
  Old times that make him smile —
For the songs he sings tell a simple tale
  Of a life that has seemed worthwhile.

1972

A Winter Morn

When the sun comes out on a winter morn
The heart is glad and you feel reborn.
A few errant clouds in a delft-blue sky
Are wisps of wonder to the questing eye,
And the soul reaches up like a bird on the wing
And a song is born as you start to sing.
Oh this is the day that the Lord has made,
Rejoice and be glad as the Psalmist said
And thank the Lord in grateful prayer
That He made this day for you to share.

1984

To Delight a Friend

One day I plucked a pretty rose
And took it to a friend.
She seemed so delighted
I tho't her thanks would never end.

She held it close in trembling hands.
She breathed its sweet perfume.
She said its color cheered her up
And chased away the gloom.

How often we neglect to give
Some simple little gift
Or say a word of love and cheer
To give some heart a lift.

Oh help us, Lord, to never miss
The little deed to cheer
Or loving word to warm the heart
And prove that you are near.

A Pebble

You may be only a pebble —
    But a pebble cast into the pool of Life —
    Where will the ripples end?
        Where will they end?

A State of Mind

Thinking wind and storm and rain?
    Think of all the sunshine after.
Thinking woes, and tears, and pain?
    Think of music and of laughter.
Thinking hopes that were in vain?
     Think of new joys you can capture.

A Rainbow Can Be Made

Do not let the weather make or mar your day
Do not let the raindrops wash your smiles away
Do not let the snowflakes cool your heart's warm glow
But smile to drive the clouds away
                and all the world will know
That God is in the raindrops as well as in the sea,
And back of every cloud the sun still shines its mystery
And God is in the sunbeam as well as in the shade
And out of every teardrop a rainbow can be made.

Coffee Break

When you think you are weary of working,
And the smallest of tasks you are shirking,
It is time, while some coffee you're drinking,
To sit down and take stock of your thinking.

Feet of Clay

My soul goes forth on steadfast wings
In search of brighter better things.
It lights my inspirations sure
It lifts my aspirations pure
My heart and thought rise true and clean
Above the fields where mortals glean,
And I would follow — up — away —
But, oh, my feet are made of clay.

1925

The Little Things

How fast the little things fill up the day
    Stealing along the hours as if they meant
    By fair or foul designing to prevent
The master deed to monument our way.
The glorious deed that might somehow portray
    The inner spirit's surge magnificent
    To tell its dream; to know one hour spent
In such a gesture that the world would say
    'Twas hero blood that flowed along his veins.
    But let us meet the little tasks with grace
    And count them as but mounting ladder bars
    And we shall learn before the morning wanes
    That by them we have climbed to such a place
    That all the little things are shining stars.

Dauntless Spirit

Eighteen

You are lovely shyly standing
　At the door to Womanhood,
Questioning the new Tomorrow:
　What is Wisdom? What is Good?

From the portals newly opened
　Earnestly you seek the way —
Looking out upon the pathways
　Leading from this brief Today.

Choose your way and step forth bravely.
　Let Life test your Faith and Heart,
Strengthen every living fibre —
　Like the bow tensed by the dart.

Life is full of shining promise
　You must hasten to fulfill,
Full of laughter and of sorrow —
　Challenges to test your will.

So, step out into adventure —
　Be undaunted by the new.
Life is good to those who meet it
　With a Faith steadfast and true.

1950

Her Hands

Her hands were never beautiful
        But capable
And vital with some hidden alchemy
        Of sympathy
That thrilled me through and through.
Those fingers never traced my brow
        But that, somehow,
The latent fires within me stirred
        As if they heard
Strange music through the mist.

No years can dull the potency
        Of memory
To move my soul to their supreme command
        To understand
As if they still were here.

If heaven perpetual youth reveals
        And age conceals
It might be I should find her there,
        A stranger fair,
And know her not again.

But let me feel her hands: I know
        No heavenly glow
Can rob them of the power they had for me
        And I shall see
And know her by her hands.
Those hands that never were beautiful
        But capable

And vital with some hidden mystery
    Of energy
That death could not destroy.

1930

Be Not Afraid

Be not afraid —
    This new experience
    That comes to you
Is not a cross that you must bear
    But a great privilege —
    Life's greatest gift —
That God has granted you may share.

Be not afraid —
    For lo! This unknown vale
    That you must cross
Is but the shadowed vale of pain
    Thru which you soon will pass
    To feel that such
Could scarce have earned so rich a gain.

Be not afraid —
    Along this oft trod path
    All Motherhood has passed
Since dawn of earth's first day
    To its divine reward.
    The vale is safe
For God — all wise — ordained the way.

Mother

You looked so sad as I left you,
    Oh, so ill and worn beside,
I was sorry, dear, to leave you,
    My place is at your side.

And I know it, dearest Mother,
    And my heart is gripped with fears,
That for leaving when you need me,
    I will pay in future years.
Pay for the lost chance to aid you,
    Help to give you proper care,
Help you in a thousand ways
    To ease the burdens that you bear.

For your health was lost in giving
    To your children through the years;
They have added to your burdens,
    Caused you heartaches, many tears.
But I know that you forgive them,
    For a mother always does,
Always finds a way to pardon
    All the hurts from those she loves.

But life is a hard taskmaster
    And I've learned the lesson true,
Learned the value of a mother
    Through pain — as you learned it too.
So remember, dearest Mother,
    As you sit, perhaps alone,
You have loves's understanding
    From the daughter you have born.

Forgotten

When someone sings "Forgotten"
 When lights are burning low
And memories come winging
 From the days of long ago
To my heart there comes such longing
 I don't know what to do
When someone sings "Forgotten"
 And I remember you.

When someone sings "Forgotten"
 Through years that are so long
I seem to hear you singing
 Once again that old sweet song
And my heart aches with such longing
 I don't know what to do
When someone sings "Forgotten"
 And I remember you.

When someone sings "Forgotten"
 The past is as today
All the peace the years have given
 By its music swept away
And my heart breaks with such longing
 I don't know what to do
When someone sings "Forgotten"
 And I remember you.

Old?

You say I am growing old.
   Perhaps I am
   if all you see
   are hairs of gray
   or less spring in
   my slower step —
   as I go my way.
But how does one judge
   what is old?
Of course we can count up
   the years for our age:
But who says that means
   that you are old?

A good wine is judged
   by the span of its years.

When the heart still can thrill
   to youth of today —
   and the morrow looms
   hopeful and bright —
When the laughter of children
   brings joy to your heart —
   and their sorrows
   can move you to tears —
When Life still has meaning
   and Love is still growing
Then how can it be
   in such joy of living
   that one is supposed
   to be Old?

Well, maybe I am
    if you reckon that Old
    is told by the passing of years.

But writing the record
    of what makes life worth living
Age doesn't matter at all.

1982

Just for Today

Just for today —
    I will not hide away in the dark closets
    of what has been,
    I will open wide the windows of my mind
    to the blessings of this day.

Just for today —
    I shall not live again my yesterdays
    but let my mind seek the promise of tomorrow.
    The intrusive wraiths of the past
    shall not shut my mind against this day.

Just for today —
    I shall open up my heart to new friends,
    new activities, new hopes for tomorrow.
    I shall know that darkness is not
    when there is light.

Just for today —
    Lord, let your light drive out
    the shadows of my yesterdays.

1975

The Gypsy Call

I shall go down the winding lane
   Just as the dusk is falling,
And out upon the bracken moor
   In answer to its calling.

And I'll forget these close white walls,
   The long dark hours of taming;
The wind shall set my tresses free
   And loose my wild blood's flaming.

I'll match my love of Romany
   In all of passion's scheming;
O I shall walk the gypsy trail —
   But only in my dreaming.

1931

To a Certain Little Lady
on Her Ninety-first Birthday

Your hands, Little Lady so weary of time,
   Let me hold them and read you
      a new birthday rhyme.
No, it's not filled with wishes for long years to come,
   But full of assurance that soon you'll be home.

Here dear, let me fix you. There, that is the way
   To rest, and remember a happier day.

* * * * *

Remember the day, O so long, long ago
    When your sweetheart first told you
            that he loved you so;
And that other bright day when you stood at his side
    So proud and yet humble to be his fair bride.
And the home that he builded so gladly for you,
    And the joys and the sorrows you met there
            — you two —
Remember the day when the first tiny head
    Was laid at your side on the clean, snowy bed;
How fragile and perfect the wee miracle seemed
    As you leaned there above it —
            the dreams that you dreamed!

Ah, the years have been kind, have been hard,
            have been long,
But your brave, dauntless spirit
            has faced them with song.
So — grieve not for the past, dear,
            the days that are gone —
    Remember the morrow, the bright, golden dawn
When the portals will open, the messenger comes
    To bring you the summons:
            Dear tired heart, come home.

                * * * * *

But — smile, Little Lady — too solemn we seem,
    'Tis not good for mortals too long thus to dream;
There, dear — brave as ever —
            I must be away —
Good bye — and, God bless you —
            a peaceful birthday.

1935

The Blind Widow Dreams

Gone is the hand that held mine in the darkness,
    Gone is the voice that stilled my every fear,
The footsteps timed to guide my faltering footsteps,
    The heart that held my heart of all most dear.

Gone my beloved, and yet behind my weeping
    There burns a brightness death can never dim
Fed by the memory of his staunch affection —
    The long brave years that I have shared with him.

There is no power to hold the heart in bondage,
    No grave so deep can hold love from its will;
There is no night because his hand is reaching
    Across the dark to guide my footsteps still.

1950

Three Ages

Youth

Love, like a wanderer, sang outside my bower.
I tho't some roving minstrel this to please me
            For an hour,
And I went forth and joined him as he sang
            Within the garden shade;
And for a time its perfume seemed more sweet
As 'neath its trees, midst flowers bright and fair,
            He rested at my feet

And sang the songs that all hearts love to hear
                And sweetest music made.
I list the wondrous tales he had to tell
As o'er my garden, for one dreamy hour,
                He cast a spell;
But still I knew him not and lightly asked,
                "Where dost thou go?"
He looked into my eyes then turned away,
His song was hushed, the garden stilled,
                Less bright the day.
He might have dwelt there had I asked him in —
                I'll never know.

Experience

Then one rode up who boldly knocked the door,
With gay commanding, called to me and I
                Stepped forth once more;
With matchless charm he smiled and as he spoke
                My heart was thrilled,
As with the magic lure he knew so well.
He painted pictures of the golden love
                He sought to tell,
And sweet each promise I so loved to hear.
                What e'er he willed
Seemed but the thing that I most longed to do,
For I was charmed and in my heart I tho't
                I love him true;
And so he tarried in the garden there.
                As time went on
The courtly lover passed and in his stead
The cruel master, and my heart oft wished
                That it were dead,
'Til wearied of my love he rode away and I
                Was left alone.

Wisdom

And then came one with quiet, courtly mien.
The door that I tho't closed to all
          Was opened again
And earnest, kindly eyes looked into mine,
          My hand was clasped;
He bowed above me with a kingly air
And long he searched my face
          Alined with care,
'Neath scars of grief the beauty of the soul
          Beheld at last;
For here was one that gravely understood
My loneliness and sought to share
          My solitude.
I bowed my head, my eyes were filled with tears,
          The pain was o'er
That long had held my heart in deep regret,
The past and all the weary way
          I must forget,
With humbled heart I asked him in
          And closed the door.

Wings of Love

As I Would Like to Do

Did you heed that little breeze
    As it passed you today, my dear,
As it paused to gently kiss your cheek
    And whisper in your ear?
I had charged it with a message,
    A word of love for you,
Had bade it linger at your side,
    As I would like to do.

I hoped that you would know, dear,
    That I had sent it there,
And wish that I were with you
    As it gently stirred your hair.
So I told it when it found you
    To say that I love you,
And leave a kiss upon your lips
    As I would like to do.

Here and There

So calmly can I think of you,
    My tranquil thought can bring to view
Without the slightest perturbations
    Such cheerful casual conversations:
Philosophy, psychology, and even introspections,
    And spicing up the whole anon
        with whimsical reflections.
Romantic love — the old and new —
        the strength of its attractions
Platonic love — the false and true —
        its certain satisfactions;
The things we've had, the things we have,
        and even what we're missing,
And settle in an abstract way
        the fallacy of kissing.
— But that's from here.

For all my calmness slips away,
    My well laid plans the truant play;
My heart rebels at dissertations,
    At useless, casual, conversations.
Philosophy, psychology and all such
        vain distractions
Are swept aside — remembering —
    The joy of love's exactions;
Remembering our yesterdays and
        finding it ironic
That I had thought that pain would die
        behind a mask Platonic.

Beneath your voice I hear the call of all
        that we are missing
And know that I was mad to think
        there was no need for kissing.
— When you are near.

1929

Gardens

Years ago as we would roam
About the garden of my home
We named each dear old-fashioned flower
After some golden love-lit hour.
But like those flowers love passed away
Leaving us only the wintry day.

But in my heart, high-walled, deep-hidden,
To which no guest is ever bidden,
I built again this garden where
Those dear old-fashioned flowers fair,
Emblems of dreams of long ago,
May bloom undimmed in time of snow.

And oft at night by the light of dreams
I walk in my garden and it seems
That time rolls back to that dear, dear past
And hand in hand we walk at last
Along that path of love-lit hours
Among those dear old-fashioned flowers.

Wanderlust

My love lies sleeping beside me,
   (And O but my love is fair)
Her lips are a flame-kissed fragrance,
    And the moonlight on her hair
Makes a web of silken meshes . . .
    And my heart is captive there.

But far strange names are calling,
    And my feet will heed the cry,
For the restless beat of the ocean
    When the night wind whispers by
Is more than the voice of a Circe
    Where distant islands lie.

'Tis the warp and woof of my being,
    And the gypsy urge beside,
Of all that sends men roving
    Over hill and dale and tide.
I must go where the strange names beckon
    And I will not be denied.

I must know the far road's windings
    That lead to Mandalay,
To Bangalore and Singapore,
    And on to old Cathay.
To Samarkand, and Ispahan
    My gypsy feet must stray.

I must go while my love lies sleeping
    (For O my love is dear)
And I could not leave if those gallant eyes
    Were dim with a parting tear;
And those soft white arms about me
    Forever would hold me here.

I must leave my loved one sleeping,
    (She sleeps so sweetly . . . still);
I must be far when the new day dawns
    Over the distant hill.
But I'll leave my heart behind me
    When I yield to the gypsy will.

Love

Oh, this shall be the way of it,
The word shall flip
In carelessness
From lip to lip
Tonight, and even
Tomorrow.

And that shall be the end of it,
And we shall part;
But one will wear
A careless smile,
And one
A broken heart.

1929

In Bondage

"Oh Life," I cried, "Grant a boon to me!"
Said Life: "O, What would you have it be?"

"Oh, send me Love, my heart to awake,
That I of its magic may partake —
The clinging arms, heart beat to heart,
Lips pressed to lips and loath to part,
Sense-reeling glance, the whispered word,
The pain of joy when the heart is stirred!"

Said Life: "If I grant this boon to thee
Great is the price you must pay to me."

"I care not for price for I am young,
My soul is brave, my heart is strong.
Oh Life, do what you will with me
Except — an empty Memory!"

Life gave the Love I asked — for a day —
Was it worth the price that I must pay?
Can a day be worth a thousand years
Of desolate hours, of secret tears?
A thousand years when Memory
Stalks through each night 'til Eternity!
A thousand years to pay! to pay!
Stretching ahead, away — away —

I called to Life: "I have paid and paid,
'Til my heart grows faint, my soul afraid!"

"But you bartered all for Love," Life cried,
"Now you must pay 'til I'm satisfied."

"Oh Life, your willing slave I'd be
Could I but empty Memory!"

A Dream

Last night I dreamed that you were here,
    That I was not alone,
Your heart, your smile, your loving words,
    Were not forever gone.

The door of happiness opened wide,
    Breathless my heart peered through
And saw the stairs of future years
    And climbed them, dear, with you.

And as we climbed your eyes met mine,
    You smiled and spoke to me,
Or gave me aid I needed not,
    So light my heart with thee.

I soared on wings of love; so bright
    Like gold, the stairs did seem;
In joy I sought to touch your hand —
    And wakened from my dream.

Because of Day — Ad Finem

Slowly the dawn comes creeping,
   Creeping out of the east;
Sadly the stars are weeping,
   Weeping that night hath ceased.
Dimly I hear them calling,
   Calling, "We must away,"
Softly their tears are falling,
   Falling because of day.

Slowly the dawn comes creeping,
   Creeping out of the east;
Softly my heart is weeping,
   Weeping that dreams have ceased.
Faintly my dreams are sighing,
   Sighing, "We must away,"
Lonely, my heart is crying,
   Crying because of day.

I Wonder

I wonder, dear, when crimson suns are setting
If you are e'er reminded by the sight
Of hours we raced into that scarlet glory
To share the splendor from some mountain height.

I wonder, too, when silver moons are drifting
Across the mystic beauty of the night
If you are e'er reminded in your dreaming
Of hours we shared the magic of their light.

I wonder, dear, when happy hearts are singing
If from your lips a song that once we knew
Will spring again and bring a tender memory
Of times I sang some old love song for you.

I wonder, too, when hearts grow old and weary,
And days drag out their length to match the years,
If by the signs of sadness you remember
That after all our gladness — there came tears.

1925

Coming Home to Ted

Dearest one, I know you're lonely,
As you sit at home alone,
But you know that it was duty's call
Or I never should have gone.
But now I am returning
And my heart is light and gay,
For soon again I'll see you,
I am coming home today!
I've been lonely too, my darling,
I have missed your many charms,
I have missed your voice, your tender smile,
And the comfort of your arms.
But the train is speeding onward
And it takes me on my way,
Oh, my heart is light and happy,
I am coming home today.

Come to Me

Come to me, oh my darling,
    As the stars shine softly above,
In the silvery light of the moonlit night
    Come to me — drink of my love.

Hold me close, oh my darling,
    Let my heart feel the beat of thine,
Oh, my Love, let me rest my head on thy breast
    As your eyes gaze into mine.

Kiss me again, oh my darling,
    Let me thrill to the fire divine,
And the wild sweet strains that surge in my veins,
    When your lips are pressed on mine.

For Love to Grow

Love does not grow like pie in the sky,
Or live on the wing like the butterfly;
Love can't grow just anywhere,
Love takes tilling, patience and care.
It needs the sunshine of happiness,
Sharing of laughter and small joys that bless;
Teardrops to soften the trials love must know,
The tenderest of care if you want it to grow.
But no joy on earth such a blessing will prove
As the happiness found in the beauty of Love.

On Receipt of Your Letter

I was so glad
When your letter came;
And first of all,
As I opened it
I saw your name;
And for a moment
I sat there
Silent,
Thinking of you.
Your dear face
Seemed to come
And smile at me
From out
The written page.

And as I read
I almost
Spoke aloud
In answer
To some thought
That you
Had written there.

You seemed so near!

The Power of Thought

Miles are as nought to the power of thought
    And Love is every where . . .
        If this is so — then we should know
        There is no Here or There . . .
    Only a happy knowing
        That you are Here
        And I am There
    Because of the Love we share.

1978

Happiness Is

Happiness shared makes the joy more sweet
And the day is brighter when two smiles meet
And hearts respond in a joy complete.
For a joy that is shared is the surest way
To gladden two hearts through another day.

1984

The Mountains — On Friendship

I have just returned from the mountains;
I wish I could make you feel the wonder of them
as I did today. They never fail to cast such
a spell over me that they no longer are just
mountains but are some Thing. And today

they were Friendship. Everywhere I went
there was written, in symbol, something of
the beauty of friendship.

First of all was their steadfastness. There
they are — no matter where I roam or how
long I am gone, when I return they are there,
unchanged.

I climbed one rugged peak, so high that
from the top it almost seemed that I could
touch the sky. And friendship often seems
like that; for after some great trial it seems
to rise in rugged strength above all else —
almost to touch the stars.

Then, wearied with my climb, I sought the
vale to list the music of the murmuring
stream, the mingled voices of the woodland
folk. There breathed the perfume, saw the
beauty of the flowers. How sweet to sit
beside a friend, to hear the music of their
voice, and hidden music of the spoken word,
to hear heart talk to heart.

I wandered on beneath great stately trees
and nought was to be heard except the gently
sighing far above among their sun-kissed
tips, as though their thoughts, in passing,
made the silence live. Oh, the majesty of
silence! Of all the blessings of friendship
I believe I like the silences the best; when
hearts pause, breathless, midst the beauty of
the thoughts. No words they need, when
soul communes with soul.

A Promise to a Wandering Friend

Whether you tramp through the far off north,
    Or travel the stormy sea,
The desert wastes, or a lonely isle,
    Or the mountains wild and free,
(For you ever will seek the solitudes
    For your heart's deep misery)
Know that my love will follow you
    Wherever you may be.

Wherever you roam I will send a thought,
    Winging the vast lone spaces through,
Straight from my heart, to seek you out,
    Bearing my tenderest love to you.

When you sit at night by your lonely tent
    And ponder your destiny,
The silent world and the distant stars,
    And the living memory
Of the shattered dreams of your once glad heart,
    Some comfort it may be
To know that a friend remembers you
    In utter sympathy.

Wherever you roam I will send a thought
    Winging the vast lone spaces through,
Straight from my heart, to seek you out,
    Bearing my tenderest love to you.

For Evelyn

Miles make no difference to the mind
For when I think of you I find
My memories bring you very near
And I am glad — you are so dear.

I see your smile — your happy face —
I feel your heart — your warm embrace —
Your love — and know though we're apart
Miles make no difference to the heart.

Where Home Is

Home is that place
   Above all others sweet,
Home is that place
   Where true hearts come to meet
   In close communion
   With the world shut out.
Home is that place
   Away from strife and doubt,
Home is that place
   Where love molds every goal
   In constant harmony
   Into the perfect whole.

1968

Father's Day

Today is devoted to honoring Father —
    Well maybe 'tis needed by some —
But to me every day is a day to remember
    The dear, blessed things he has done.

'Twas he matched his stride to the step of wee children,
    Who tenderly smiled at our joy,
Who willingly paused in the stress of his labor
    To make or to mend us a toy.

Who toiled through the years nor complained at his labor
    Nor thought any service to mind —
Who gave of his life and his strength for our pleasure
    But Father — dear, patient and kind.

Mother

No word in all the world so sweet;
No word that is so oft repeat
With love, with pride, in pain, in prayer,
From the heights of joy, the depths of care;
By the lisping babe, by the man full grown;
From the lowliest hut to the highest throne;
No word that wakes in a faltering breast
Such great desire to do its best;
That stands for a love so staunch and true
As the word, dear Mother,
    That means — just You.

1938

To My Husband — Father's Day

The days will come and the days will go
But good or ill we take them.
If they are gay, or if they are sad,
They are mostly what we make them.

So let us take each bright new day
And keep it free from sorrows,
And fill it with sweet memories
To brighten our tomorrows.

Oh, let us take this Father's Day
And fill it with such gladness
That it will be a shining light
For any morrow's sadness.

1960

Dear Daughter

For all the hours of patient care,
The big and little trials you share.
For all the things you do for me,
I'm thankful, dear, as I can be,
And wish for you in every way
A very happy special day.

1983

Your Little Notes

'Tis sad when loved ones
   have to part,
It leaves an empty place
   within the heart;
But when I find just here
   and there —
Those little love-notes
   everywhere
Loneliness seems to fade
   away
And memory recalls
   another day;
So many other days,
   my dear,
As you've grown sweeter
   year by year,
Since that first day
   until the now . . .
The first born of my only
   son, somehow —
You have given such love to me
   from babyhood to maturity.
What a joy to my heart
   you will always be.
It seems each member of
   my family
Has each some special reason
   to be dear to me.
So thank you for the notes you
   left behind
They are so very precious
   and so kind,

And such a comfort to
    a lonely heart,
And make it easier that
    we have had to part.

From Grandma

A bushel of love and a thank you, too
Is stored in this heart I send to you.

To My Son

I travelled near — I travelled far —
I went on foot — I went by car —
Until my head went round and round
And finally this one card I found
To say to you in a motherly way —
"Dear Son, a happy Father's Day."
May you reach your goal
        in each game you play.

To Peggy

In a very special way
For a very special day
We wish you lots of fun,
With health, and happiness for you
In all the things you plan to do
Now that you are Twenty-One.

Merry Christmas —
To the Folks at Home

Today you are gathered together
   and I cannot be there!
It seems as if that simple line
   is more than I can bear;
For the thought of early morning
   with the children's shouts resounding;
And the great tree in the corner
   with its precious gifts abounding;
And the hustle and the bustle,
   chattering, whispering, and confusion;
"Ohs" and "Ahs" of awe and wonder;
   papers scattered in profusion,
Wakes within my heart such longing
   to be with you on this day
That it seems I cannot bear it
   that I am so far away.

Then a thought of cheer comes stealing —
   swift the days will pass away,
Swift will pass the white-robed winter —
   then the summer's golden sway;
Then shall I the long miles vanquish,
   by the paths the birds have flown
To their own beloved northland
   to the land of Love and Home.

Now the southland holds me captive
   but my heart has sped away
Journeying with this humble message
   for a peep at you today.

All the miles that lie between us
    could not bar it from a call
Just to wish you Merry Christmas —
    "Merry Christmas one and all."

The Day After

'Tis the day after Christmas, we all feel the pressure
Of where to put things that won't stack on the dresser.

The papers are piled on the sewing room floor,
With boxes and gadgets half blocking the door,
With ribbons and bows in such tumbled profusion
How can you bring order to such wild confusion?

O well, there's tomorrow — do your best with today —
Perhaps you can get all this mess put away
In time to forget where you stored them, I fear,
When you want to get ready for Christmas, next year.

1975

Crocheted Pot Holder

Count the stitches and you will know,
If you measure the love each stitch will show,
From the very moment that you begin,
Just how much love is woven in.

1960

The Quest for Happiness

Endless the quest as the wind and tide,
    Far-ah-far as the world is wide,
But he who would find it must humble his pride
    And seek for it first at his own fireside.

1930

When Day Is Done

Home and the windows burning
With the flame of sun's last gleam
Home and the flitting swallows
Wheeling above the stream.

Home and the shadows slipping
Swiftly and long and still,
Home and the evening creeping
Down from the guardian hill.

Home and the breezes kissing
The roses beside the way
Wafting their precious incense
After the dying day.

Home and the sounds of twilight
Each one a living part,
Home — and the open doorway —
Home and the waiting heart.

Cuddlesome, Fuddlesome Things

Whimsy

Write a witty
Little ditty,
Find a happy air;
Be a silly
Happy dilly,
Sing it everywhere.

Never weary
Never teary,
Play the happy clown;
Always very
Bright and merry
Write your ditty down.

Step out lightly
Sing it brightly
Everywhere you go,
Sing it madly,
Sing it gladly
So your love will show.

Babies

Dear little cuddlesome, fuddlesome things,
With gestures as gentle as angel's wings:
Rose-petaled cheeks, and hair like down,
Little pug nose, and — blue or brown —
Bright little eyes; and lips that smile
At an angel's kiss — so free from guile.
Dear little mites of humanity,
How strong your grasp on our hearts can be;
Enriching our lives till the whole world sings —
You dear little cuddlesome, fuddlesome things.

Two Little Girls

There are two little girls named Terry and Pam
And both are as sweet as can be.
I wish I could see them and give each a kiss,
And I'm sure they would like to see me.

The big sister is Terry and she cares for Pam
And keeps her from running away,
And Pam loves her sister and watches for her
To come home from school everyday.

1961

When You Live in a House
on a Hill

There once were two children
    Named Billy and Jane
Who lived in a house on a hill,
    With a yard that went up,
    And a yard that went down,
    And a view that looked out
    On the Bay and the town,
And a road you could play on at will,
    With wagons and bikes
    And doll-buggies and trikes,
And no one to say: "Do be still!"
    All the girls and the boys
    Could make such a noise!
Oh it's fun when you live on a hill!

So Janie and Bill and a puppy or two
Kept busy from morning 'til night,
    And playmates came up
    And playmates came down
To play in a yard that looked out on the town
In a world that was sunny and bright;
    And young Bill would whistle
    And Janie would sing
And practice a gay little trill
    As they played in the yard
    That went down and went up
To the house that was built on a hill.

1947

Pot Holder

A holder for your favorite pot,
For a doily or a plate that's hot,
It is so very versatile —
Because it is reversible.

The Netscrubber

I'm a happy little scrubber
In the dishpan I'm just dandy.
For safely cleaning Teflon
You'll find me very handy.
Your every need I will fulfill
So use me freely where you will.

A Little Bag for Scrap Soap

You'll find me economical
And neat and useful too
If you'll put your scraps of soap in me
And let me work for you,
    I'll scrub your knees
    I'll scrub your toes
Your heels and elbows too,
In fact most any scrubbing job
You'll find for me to do.

1966

Two Houses

Close by the lane the little house stood
    In the shade of the sycamore tree,
While just over yonder and not far away
    The big house, disdainfully,
Looked down from her gabled immensity
    And said with her haughtiest air
Of the neat little house by the side of the lane,
    "Such neighbors! I do declare."

Proudly she looked o'er her gardens prim,
    Not a shrub nor a blossom astray,
And stretched out her manicured lawns to the curb
    In quite a self-satisfied way.
"'Some house,' said my builders, 'we've spared no expense.'
    And keep me unblemished they must,
No children shall race o'er my stairways and halls,
    Or trample my beauty to dust."

But the little house smiled at her neighbor's disdain
    In a friendly, compassionate way,
And spread out her lawns like a grandmother's lap,
    And laughed at the children at play.
She opened her windows as wide as she could
    And said to the sycamore tree,
With just the least curtsy of old-fashioned pride
    "'Some *home*,' say my neighbors of me."

The Little Brown Seed

Deep in the heart of the little brown seed
A wonderful giant lies hidden.
    As it lies on the ground
        He stirs gently 'round
With threats of arising, unbidden.

"Oh, dear!" Softly sighs the little brown seed,
"Such a headache I cannot endure,
    I shall take a wee nap
        In Mother Earth's lap
For something is wrong I am sure."

So deep in the earth the little brown seed
Slept through the snow and the rain
    Then awoke with a start
        And a pain in its heart.
The giant was stirring again.

"Oh, it is spring!" cried the little brown seed,
"I've been sleeping the whole winter through.
    I must rise from my sleep
        And go take a peep
And see what there is I can do."

"I feel so strange," said the little brown seed,
"I have arms and legs too, it would seem,
    I can reach all around
        Here under the ground,
And above I can see the sun gleam."

"This will be fun," said the little brown seed,
"For now I can scamper and play."
    "Oh, no, Little Seed,"
        Said the giant, "Indeed,
For now you must do what I say."

"Oh, but I won't," said the little brown seed,
"I have feet and I must run around."
    But the giant said, "Stay!
        You can't run and play,
I have fastened your feet in the ground."

"You must work now, dear Little Brown Seed,
You must stretch up your arms to the sun,
    And under the ground
        You must reach all around,
Oh, your work here is only begun."

And after a while the little brown seed
Looked gaily about on the world
    And children oft played
        About in its shade
While breezes its twinkling leaves whirled.

"Oh, this is great," said the little brown seed
"And I'm happy as happy can be,
    I am glad I obeyed
        What the old giant said,
It is *wonderful* to be a tree."

A *Little Tree*

Alone and lonely
    the little tree stood
Far from the edge
    of the nearest wood,
Looking out on a strange
    white world
As the soft new snowflakes
    around it swirled.
"Why am I here alone,"
    it cried:
"And so alone?" it
    softly sighed.
Gently the snowflakes
    covered its face
Till a little white angel
    stood in its place
And sheltered it from ice
    and storm
Keeping the little tree
    safe and warm
Till the winter passed
    and the little tree stood
No longer alone
    from a distant wood.
For close at its side
    with springtime's glow
A whole new forest
    for it to know
Looked out on the world from
    the earth's warm heart

Of the endless cycle
    to be a part.
And the little tree
    sighed contentedly
To be a part of such
    company.

1982

Little Brook

Little Brook, as you hurry along,
    Why do you sing such a merry song?
Why is your heart so light and gay,
    Don't you know that the day is gray?

Little Brook, as you pass the mill
    You turn the wheel with a merry trill,
You never loiter and never shirk.
    Don't you know that it is work?

Little Brook, as you gurgling pass
    Over the boulders and thru the grass,
Or leap with a laugh from the hindering bluff,
    Don't you know that the way is rough?

Little Brook, as you go your way,
    Working and playing the livelong day,
You seem to be seeking the morrow with glee.
    Don't you know of the hungering sea?

Ripples

I stood at the edge of a crystal lake
    In the calm of a summer's day
And idly tossing a pebble in
    Watched the ripples spread away.
Like swallows they flit o'er the drowsy lake
    Scarce troubling its dreaming more
'Til the last one broke with a tender smile
    Where the waters kissed the shore.

The Puddle

It had rained a little while before
    and the little puddle in the hollow by the step
    was deep . . . as deep as the sky was high,
And down in its very uttermost depths
    was pinned to the earth
    by a thousand stars.

Once Upon a Time

A hundred little pussy-cats
All fuzzy little pussy-cats,
    Came out one day in spring,
And sitting on a willow bough
A swaying, swinging willow bough
    Began to gaily sing.
And just across a little rill,
A lovely, laughing little rill

That danced upon its way,
About a hundred puppy-dogs,
All snowy, blowy puppy-dogs,
    In quite a doggy way
Began to bark and growl at them
And then to growl and bark at them,
    To scare them from their bough.
"What right have they," the puppies cried,
"To come and sing our rill beside?
    Begone!" they barked, "Right Now!"
But all those little pussy-cats,
Those saucy little pussy-cats,
    Just arched their little backs,
And said, "My dears, we'll pay no heed,
So very bad their bark, indeed,
    All melody it lacks."
And all those little pussy-cats,
Those brave and daring pussy-cats,
    Sang out with all their might;
The frantic puppies barked away
And looked as fierce as puppies may,
    As surely was their right.
But all those puppy-dogs could do,
No matter what they tried to do,
    Was bark and bark, you see,
For they were only snowy blooms
Just snowy, blowy little blooms
    Upon a dog-wood tree.
And all those little pussy-cats,
Those saucy little pussy-cats,
    Who seemed so brave to be,
Were only little fuzzy buds
Just little fuzzy satin buds
    Upon a willow tree.

A Little Robin
With Only One Leg

Once upon a time a little robin
Came to live in my backyard.
He moved into my cherry tree and there
With all his little heart he sang to me.

And I watched over him
Because — it seemed so very sad —
Although he was so cheerful
One leg was all he had.

I put out seeds to help him —
I scared away the cat —
And wondered what had happened
To cripple him like that.

I wondered if some thoughtless boy
With slingshot or a gun
Had struck him such a cruel blow
When he was out for fun.

Then as I watched him hop about
I thought — I'll never know.

But I knew that God was watching
And using even me
To help to keep him safe from harm
As he sang so cheerfully.

1979

The Old Black Crow

An old black crow sat up in a tree,
   As I went by he spoke to me,
"Caw," he cried, and I knew it was so
   That I was a joke to the old black crow.

Star Babies

The little star-babies are all rocked to sleep
In a cradle of magic both downy and deep
      That is made from the silver moon.
Then softly, ah, softly a curtain is drawn
Hiding them close from the light of the dawn
      As they sleep in the silver moon.
And all through the day while the sun passes by
Not a star-baby wakens to gurgle or cry
      As they rock in the silver moon.
But after the sunlight has gone from the skies
How quickly they open their bright little eyes
      And climb from the silver moon
And over the sky-meadows romp in delight
And play peek-a-boo with the shadows of night
      That watch by the silver moon.
Till daylight appearing, they creep back once more
All tired and sleepy across the sky floor
      To be rocked in the silver moon.
And softly, ah softly, a curtain is drawn
Hiding them close from the light of the dawn
      As they sleep in the silver moon.

The Sun-God

The Sun-god smiled as he slowly awoke —
    And the darkness fled away —
And said, as he peeped o'er the misty hills,
    "I must visit the world today."

So he sent forth an army of gleaming rays
    To turn the clouds to gold,
While he kissed the tips of the mountain peaks
    In a manner bright and bold.

Then he stepped in a trice o'er the eastern hills
    And smiled on all about,
Sent his radiant glance anear and far —
    The world awoke with a shout.

With his crown of gold he lighted the sky,
    But he trod the earth with his feet;
Warm was the greeting he gave to all,
    And light was his tread — and fleet.

For soon he had passed o'er the busy world
    But pausing a moment to rest
He lighted the sky with his parting smile
    Then went to his home in the west.

And over the waters a flaming path
    As far as the eye could see.
Oh this was the path the Sun-god trod
    On his way across the sea.

O Lady Moon

Where are you going, O Lady Moon,
    Fleeing away in your silver shoon,
A-trailing your robes of misty white
    Across the star-strewn path of night?

From what do you fly, O Lady Moon,
    A pirate or lover seeking a boon,
That you may not pause in your ceaseless flight
    Across the star-strewn path of night?

Birthday Greetings

Like unto a little sailboat
    Is this birthday note to thee,
Laden with a bounteous cargo
    It starts out across the sea.

And its burden is good wishes
    For success along thy road;
Precious jewels, too, of Friendship
    Are included in its load.

Kindly memories are the breezes
    That will waft it on its way,
May it safely reach its harbor,
    Bring thee joy upon this day.

Angels

I wonder if angels ever get tired,
And if they do — what do they do
If the task assigned is not yet through?
Does *my* guardian angel ever get tired?

What can I do, I wonderingly ask,
To brighten its day, to ease its task?
Perhaps I should try even better to be
So my angel can rest when it watches me.

In the Garden

I walked into my garden in the dew
To see if peas I'd planted had come through.
I was so eager — hoping they were up —
When in their midst I saw a mongrel pup.
He was so happy romping in their green,
But I felt only anger at the scene.
I called to him; he did not run in dread
But greeted me with wagging tail instead
And rushed to meet me in a friendly way —
A new-found friend to make a perfect day!
My anger passed, it had not been so strong
New peas would grow again before too long.
He had not meant my garden ground to mar,
In payment offered love to heal the scar.
I could not send his pleading eyes away —
I took him in — he is my friend today!

1974

Memories

Yesterday

The old West is almost gone,
Nothing is as it was when I was young.
Covered wagons, cattle roundups
And country dances — with an old fiddler
Sitting in a chair on the kitchen table;
The one room schoolhouse where each child
Learned all the lessons as his own.
And evenings when we sat on the porch
Listening to the music from a drifting boat,
Or sitting around the lamp in the old livingroom
While Mother read aloud from well-loved magazines.

Childhood Fancies

When I was a child, on a moonless night,
After the heat of a summer's day,
I would sit on a log of the great woodpile
My father had brought 'gainst the winter's needs,
And wait for the flash of the Northern lights;
And ever they came — a flash — and gone,
Over and over in the still night air.

My childish fancy saw over the hills
A monstrous giant crouching down,
And ever raising his beetling brows
To peer o'er the ridge of the encircling hills,
And the light that flashed was the terrible ray
Of his fiery eyes as he glanced about,
Then quickly low'ring his brow again
Left me alone in the velvet dark.

I always wondered what it was he saw
In that flashing glance he cast on the world —
Did he see a wee child watching there?
And if he did, did he smile or frown?
And I would tremble in the warm night air,
As I list the various sounds of night:
The cattle that stirred in the field nearby —
Strange black shapes in the throbbing dark —
The horses that stamped on the stable floor;
A coyote's cry from a lonely copse;
A night bird's screech on the river bank.

The voices echoing from out the house,
Hidden from me by the old woodshed,
Seemed strange, unreal and far away,
And I was afraid, but I dared not leave,
Held by the lure of those beetling brows
And the lightning flash, in the eerie sky,
Of those terrible eyes as they looked at me.

How glad I would be when someone called
And said it was time to go to bed.

Yet every night when the moon was dark
I would go and sit on the old woodpile —
A wee dreaming tot alone in the night —
And wait for the giant to peep at me
Over the dark mysterious hills,
And shiver and thrill in ecstasy.

Interlude

The heavy scent of sagebrush fills the air
As cowboys urge the noisy, worried cattle
Past the lonely one room schoolhouse,
Where the faces of little children,
                        like cut-out paper masks,
Press against dusty window panes.
The hours in school will seem less long today.

Scrapbag

I emptied my mother's scrapbag
Out on the snowy cover
Of the guest room bed
And I smiled in contemplation
    of the mess
To think how she had hoarded
Every tiny bit of ribbon,
    cloth and lace.

And then I thought
Of all my dresser drawers
The cabinets, the sewing room,
Upstairs, the basement, the garage —
My odds and ends were not in
    just one bag
And so I sought to organize
    my scraps.

The job is done
But I have just begun
For sorting out that sad array
I find by introspection
That my mind is more like
    Mother's scrapbag
Than my house.

How can I know just what
    to cast away,
Just what to store,
Just what will someday
    meet a need
Or be a burden more.

As fragile as a spider's web
A thread of memory
That might weave a lovely
Pattern for tomorrow's need
Or prove to be a bitterness
That I must weed.

Chiaroscuro

How oft the scenes of yesteryear
    By time and distance kissed
In fragrant, happy memories
    Come stealing through the mist.
Chameleon to fit the mood
    The memory wafts along
Of one that sped on silver wings
    And brought my heart a song.
And one there was invoked the dawn,
    Entrapped its rosy gleam
And wove a mantle for desire
    And left my heart a dream.
And one that walked the star-shot night
    A moonbeam for a staff,
That whispered through the purple deeps
    And brought my heart a laugh.
Yet one more dear than all the rest
    Strikes down athwart the years,
The swift sweet memory of you,
    The one that brought me tears.

1928

The Picnic

It was a lovely afternoon
    to go for a ride
As my friends and I
    in a happy mood
Took the winding road
    towards Mt. Hood.
Soon the Valley
    with rivers and towns
Was lost to our view
    but the road unwound
To scenes anew
    and every turn
Was fresh delight
    with only the sound
Of our purring car
    to ruffle the peace
That was everywhere.
    And everywhere
    the world seemed right.
We threaded our way
    to a lovely spot
Where Camp Creek tumbled
    over twig and rock,
Murmuring its happy
    mountain song
To the summer sky
    as it hurried along.
We picnicked there
    in the shady glen.
We chatted a happy time
    and then

We had our lunch —
    it was, oh, so good —
There in the shade
    of the sylvan wood.
For a table we had
    the stump of a tree
For music — the waters
    flowing by,
The breeze in the branches
    overhead
And the song of a bee
    in a flower nearby.
So lovely and quiet
    and peaceful there,
We refreshed our souls
    in the mountain air
And felt that God
    is everywhere.
We felt 'made new'
    as we turned toward home
Renewed in our hearts
    for the days to come.

1982

That Night

The night that made you dear to me
The dawn that found you near to me
All linger in my dreams, sweetheart, of you.
Still linger in my dreams, sweetheart, of you.

The Mountains
From a Moving Train

I boarded the train my heart rampant with the
pain and rebellion of parting from loved ones —
the cruel pain that grips the heart as in a vise and
blinds the eyes with unshedable tears — tears that
must be swallowed back to feed the pain anew.
My throat ached with the strain of speaking fare-
well words with a lilt in the voice and a smile on
the face.

And thus the hours passed — the miles sped by.
But gradually came peace; such a peace as I had
never known. For slowly the rhythm of sound and
motion crept into my heart and with it — a calm.
And memories, before the time of parting, came —
and I found myself, no longer blinded, watching
the mountains passing by. I love the mountains
and as I watched the ever flowing trees, the ever
changing scenes became to me a Symbol. My
grief was stilled; my heart slipped into the past and
lived again.

The ever flowing trees became the constant
current of my life. Here one, a rare and verdant
green — a lovely memory, a deed well done; here
one so frail, yet struggling to grow — some weak-
ness which my heart has striven to overcome,
still strives yet has not won, else strong and healthy
it would be; here stands one dead — some error I
have made — yet even as the leaves of this dead

tree have gone to feed anew the bright green foliage
'bout its feet so does my error teach and even, by
contrast, brighten better deeds that have it hedged
about — perhaps in hopes that none may see.

And like the tree that dies, yet gaunt ghost,
stands there yet, my errors — dead — still reach
their ghostly fingers forth and strum the harp of Life,
and through the lilting music of happy memories
I hear their minor strain.

Just now we crossed a burned and barren waste
— how quick I see a stretch of wasted years. Now
gone — more trees — why, I could almost name
each one, so real to life they seem. Ah! there a
mountain stream — how plain I see one beauteous
thread of memory that runs through all the years —
a lovely sparkling stream. Sometimes 'tis almost
lost among the vines and weeds. Ah, there it
comes again!

I fain would linger by this stream, to hear it
murmuring to me the things my heart would love
to hear, but we rush on. And yet I know that when
the mountains are behind, this self-same stream
will follow too, and even as I, must still go on.

And suddenly I realize my thoughts have passed
from memory to future hopes and plans, and peace
and calm possess my heart — rebellion stilled —
and still the train moves on. But now I feel that
miles are naught to those who love and trust.
The mountains have shared with me their enduring
serenity, their message is in my heart, the trees —
the stream — flow on.

The Midnight Express

A low, deep rumble and into sight,
Splitting the beauty of the night,
Sweeps an iron monster with gleaming eye,
Sending against the starry sky
The long black line of its mighty breath —
An angel of mercy, a demon of death.
Shattering the silence, blast on blast,
With a savage roar it rushes past.

The darkness closes on every side,
The silence swells like an inborn tide,
And suddenly out of the night is heard
The small complaint of a sleepy bird.

1928

Today

No horses to care for —
No hired man.
Then like a movie cutting back to now
The scenery shifts to a scene today
And I see my neighbor coming home
From an office job at the close of the day
And his young wife watches him from their door
And I see the children run in from their play
And I wonder if life means the same to him
Here in the town at the end of the day.

Let Love Fill Their Vacant Place

Love's Solace

When a loved one passes from you
    And your memories you trace
Let the joys you shared together
    Dry the teardrops from your face.
Do not waste time in regretting
    Let love fill their vacant place.

1976

Requiem

One by one the blossoms' petals fall,
One by one the roses fade and die,
One by one the leaves fall from the trees,
Leaving an empty place against the sky.

The footsteps falter and the eyes grow dim
As one by one the relentless days depart
And one by one old friends go on before
Leaving an empty place within the heart.

1976

A Gift of Time

It is not easy
When first you think on Death
But when you think with reason
Upon the joy and miracle of birth —
The gift of Breath — a life's beginning,
A gift of time to live and love
      Upon this earth —
It seems unreasonable for one
To think there is no end
For as Love brought you into being
So Love — your journey done —
      Will call you home.

A Trilogy

I   Before Death

When God reaches forth His hand
    And says to me "Come"
Let no man's hand
    With pump and tubes
    And alien fluids
Hold me back
    Or seek to push
    God's hand away.
His will is mine
Let no one come between.

II   Death

If this be Death
    Then do not grieve for me,
And do not seek to hold me back . . .
    Let me be free.
The way that opens on ahead
Is bright with light no sun
    Has ever made. It draws me on.
    It draws me on in rhythmic beauty
        To a music not yet heard.
    If this be death . . .
        Then do not grieve for me.

Ahead I see a room so beautiful
My heart stands still
      Such beauty to behold.
And I can see some happy people move
      About the room as if to ready it
For some new guest. I look around
But no one can I see. Then suddenly I know
That room they are preparing is for me!
      If this be death . . .
          Then do not grieve for me.

You take my hand and seek
      To hold me back — O, let me go.
I must move on. I would be one
      Of those who wait for me . . .
I would be one of those
Who serve the Lord.

I served Him here, but now
I would move on to where He waits
To welcome one who yearns
      To serve Him there.

The light enfolds me now —
There is no dark behind —
In joy I reach and touch
      My Savior's hand.
If this be death . . .
      Then do not grieve for me.

III After Death —
    The Prisoner

    You grieve above my grave
        And think that I
    Rebellious in the tomb
        Imprisoned lie.

    If I could grieve in this celestial
        Bliss
    Then I should grieve for you
        Who grieve for me:
    If I could speak across the
        Bright abyss
    Then I should tell you:
        Leave my poor grave be.

    'Tis mockery you should weep there.
        Till you die
    You are the prisoner bound,
        Dear one, not I.

1930

Untitled

Gathering flowers for the Master's bouquet
Dear little flowers that will never decay,
Gathered by angels and carried away
To blossom forever in the Master's bouquet.

Memories

Like a ghost you rise before me
    Wherever I may go,
Your sweet smile haunts my memory
    And O, I want you so.

You are with me in the morning
    When first I see the light,
Your dear voice echoes softly
    As I close my eyes at night.

In every crowd I seem to see
    Your dear and smiling face,
And near me, as I sit alone,
    You come and take your place.

O, the way is far less lonely,
    As the years a-past me glide,
To know that, even in memory,
    You are ever at my side.

My Sister

Thou player on the thousand stringed harp,
    Thy sweet celestial strains reached even here
And softly echo in each lonely heart
    Of those on earth who held thy presence dear,
And bids them wait in peace for God's own will
    And gives them strength to bravely carry on,
Complete the given span of life until
    God bids thee reach thy hand to guide them home.

How Can I Live Without You

For you, dear, my heart is ever yearning
To you, dear, my thoughts are ever turning
    — back to the past.
When I sit in the twilight and dream
    — dream of the long ago.
In the mist that drift and spread
    — in seeming endlessness —
Through the weary night the memories come winging
Tender words of love dear, they are ever bringing
    — that could not last.

How can I live with out you, dear
How can I face the empty years
How can I learn to bear their pain
And dry my tears and to smile again
How can I learn to bear the loss
How can I learn to kiss the cross
Without you, dear, what shall I do
Oh how can I live without you?

1972

A Message to Nellie

In memories you come to us
In memory we keep you near
We walk again where once we walked
And talk of things we held most dear.

The Quest

The Hall of Life is dimly lit.
Man, looking back, sees but a brief way into it,
About him, one small chamber called Today,
Ahead, Tomorrow's mystery dims the way.
While from the encircling gloom he faintly hears
The echoing footsteps of the passing years
      Upon the earthy floor.

He knows not whence he came nor whither bound,
But ever seeking . . . ever thinking he has found . . .
He hastens on. Tomorrow's mystery pales,
Becomes Today, and in the past re-veils
      In shadow deep once more.

And ever that faint dimming in the shadow lures him on
Toward distant heights for which his soul seems born;
Some hidden faith forever springs anew:
Some hidden hope that he may live to view
The glorious fount from which all life must flow;
That he may pierce the veil, the end to know;
Yet even as he seeks . . . death overtakes,
      The quest is done

      . . . Or is it just begun?

      Or is it just begun . . . ?

1929

Lord — Take My Hand

My Creed

I would be kind consistently
Not pick and choose
To whom, nor when
I would extend that fellowship
That sets man from the lesser kind
A thing apart,
In partnership with One divine.

I would be kind consistently
Ignoring not
This call or that,
Nor heeding it be night or day
A need shall fall across my path
And give me chance
To work with Him for "one of these."

My God

Mine is a Living God —
   Lord, let me be
   Worthy the gift of life
   You gave to me.

Mine is a Loving God —
   Lord, let me be
   A channel, that this precious gift
   May flow through me.

Mine is a Trusting God —
   Lord, let me see
   A way to trust my fellowman
   As you trust me.

Mine is a Mighty God —
   Lord, make me strong
   To meet the challenge of each day
   And do no wrong.

Mine is a Forgiving God —
   Lord, let me find
   The love to cancel other's debts
   As you have mine.

Mine is an Understanding God —
   Who knows my need;
   Help me another's cares to meet
   By word and deed.

Mine is an Everpresent God —
    And hushed and still
    I wait with willing mind and heart
    To learn His will.

1974

Take My Hand

Lord — take my hand.
    I stumble
And tomorrow seems less sure.

I need you, Lord.
    Sometimes
The way seems dark
    The spider of fear
Spins a web of doubt
    About me
As the tides of life
    Begin to ebb.

Lord — take my hand
    And lead me
Out of the threatening shadows
    Into thy precious light.

Lord — take my hand.

1982

If a Miracle Should Happen for You

Once upon a time in the long ago
    Some shepherds watching their flocks by night
Were suddenly awed by a brilliant light
    And an angel telling a wondrous story
While an angel choir sang a song of glory
    And the shepherds, believing, hurried away
To see the Christ child where he lay
    In his humble cradle — in the hay.

If you were a shepherd watching your flock
    In the half-way black of a starlit night
What would you do?
    If suddenly a strange white light
Slanted down from the distant stars
    Across the dark — to touch the earth
And bathe your flock — your flock and you —
    In its awesome light,
        What would you do?

Would you run away, or watch the
    Bright beams winnowing in strange array
As if they were stirred by unseen wings,
    While the night was filled with heavenly song —
And suddenly there in the light there stood
    An angel throng.
        What would you do?

And if an angel spoke to you
    From that light so bright you could hardly see —

And told you a tale that was wondrous strange.
    Would you believe
And hasten to see
    That the story was true?

If a miracle should happen to you
    What would *you* do?
            What *would* you do?

The Omen

A mother dreamed by a manger bed
    As her fingers tousled a downy head
And her eyes gazed out through the stable door
    To where a star slipped lower . . . lower . . .
Till it hung like a lamp above the door.

Her eyes grew wide at the light it shed
    On the fair young face in the manger bed,
And her dreams leapt out beyond the door,
    But the star came on, slipped lower . . . lower . . .
Till it stood like a cross before the door.

And the mother's heart stood still with dread,
    As she visioned the pathway His feet must tread,
The pathway that led from the stable door,
    But the star came on, slipped lower . . . lower . . .
Till it burned like a crown at the stable door.

1935

The Reward of Service

'Tis not in vain man serves his fellowman
If one of these in some far distant day
In looking backward down the grooves of time
Remembers one that helped him on the way.

Just this alone reward enough would be,
That one still keeps the memory of your hand,
That just one heart grown strong should pause to say:
Remember how you helped me understand?

But more than this shall be his sure reward
Who shares his love and strength to meet their needs,
Who lifts his brothers' burdens with his Faith,
For Heaven itself keeps records of these deeds.

'Tis not in vain man serves his fellowman,
'Tis not in vain man stoops to lift his load,
'Tis not in vain man slows his swifter stride
To walk beside some brother down the road.

For when the race, though swift or slow, is run
And man shall come to his accounting day
And angels search the records of the past
The totals shall be balanced in this way:

So many times he missed his chosen dream
Because he helped another to his goal,
So many times his own cares thrust aside
To carry cheer to some unhappy soul.

So many times he turned from his desire
To guide some little footsteps to the light

Remembering the "unto one of these"
Of One who walked this troubled world aright.

Of these the searching angels shall take note,
And all the other records shall grow dim
Before the glory of the written word:
"As to the least of these — so unto Him."

All else is naught. This is the record judged.
The Alpha and Omega of God's Plan.
And lo! The man shall hear them bid him pass —
'Tis not in vain man serves his fellowman.

Empathy

When you are wounded by some unkind word
Drown not yourself in pity for your pain
But look with mercy on the troubled one
Caught in the web of fancied persecution.
Forgive — and seek to help them love again.

Remember Christ when on the cross He hung
Surrounded by unbridled hue and cry
Thought only of their tragedy and sin
And prayed not for himself amid the din
But said "Before I go, dear Father God,
    Forgive them for they
        know not what they do.
    Forgive them for they
        know not what they do."

1979

When Jesus Walked

When Jesus walked in Galilee
    Along the dusty way
The little children came to watch
    And hear what he would say.

The men who walked with Jesus there
    Said, "Let the Master be,
He has important things to do
    And people He must see."

But Jesus said, "Forbid them not."
    And took them on his knees,
"My Father claims them as his own
    And Heaven is made for these."

If you would walk the Jesus way —
    So strong — so good — so mild —
You must renounce your world-wise ways
    And be a seeking child.

1977

On Loneliness

Today I stood alone in a crowd;
    And while I know He is everywhere,
    It seemed as if God wasn't there,
The voice of the many was so loud.

When later I stood on the crest of a hill
     That "still small voice" was in the air,
     It seemed that God was everywhere
And loneliness fled at my Savior's will.

An Evening Prayer

The night is upon me, Lord —
     The day is done.

How have I used this gift of time?
There have been wasted moments
     But I have tried.
I listened for your guiding voice, dear Lord,
     In all I did.
But if I missed some messages —
     (Or did not follow through)
Forgive me, Lord, and let me walk
     Another day with you.

But whether I did well or ill
     I thank you, God,
For this day, and the love
     You let me share.
I shall rest well this night
     In your dear care.

     In Jesus' Name,
                    Amen

1975

A Prayer — Answered

Lord, let me walk the high road,
   And let me grope the low,
And let me drift on the misty flats,
   The better that I may know
The sorrows and joys of my fellowmen,
   That I may help them the better then.

Lord, let me talk with old hearts,
   And let me love with young,
And let me play with the little ones,
   And understand their tongue;
Lord, let me learn from the speech of all,
   That I may answer them when they call.

Lord, let me sing the glad song,
   And let me know despair,
And let me chant with the common folk
   Their day's monotonous air;
Let me know the hurt of a hushed refrain
   That I may help them to sing again.

*　*　*　*　*

Lord, I have walked the high road,
   And I have groped the low,
And been adrift on the misty flats,
   And now I know — I know —
The infinite need of my fellowmen,
   And I thank Thee, Lord.
            Amen! Amen!

1927

Acknowledgements

Special thanks are extended to Evelyn Alquist, Steven Cielinski, Mary Jane Ferris, and the many others who helped to make this book possible. Contributions toward the production and publication were made by the following friends and family of Janie Byrnes:

Clara Abrams — Amy Kahle Ackerman — Paul Ackerman
Nancy Aleck — Evelyn Alquist — Arlene Anderson
Eunice Zachary Arnold — Edna Atwood — Violet Beck
Dave and Roberta Brown — Terrence and Peggy Byrnes
Pamela Byrnes — Terry Byrnes and John Finger
Jonathan Byrnes Finger — Iris Byrnes Finger — Gladys Chalk Pierce
Gene and Julie Chapin — Anna Chapin — Debbi Chapin Climer
Bob Cielinski — James and Susan Cielinski — Jane Cielinski
Steven and Lori Cielinski — Chelsie Cielinski
Christopher Cielinski — Viola Clark — Edward and Mona Clark
Dick and Mary Ann Crites — Beatrice Darnall — Marian Dodge
Jonathan and Debra Doty — Donald and Evelyn DuRette
Zella Durisch — Ken and Lorraine Dworschak
James and Peggy Earle — Catharine Edmark — Cathren Eversole
Melton and Mary Jane Ferris — Toni and George Finger
Don and Olive Frazier — Irene and Jerry Fritzke — Hazel Gardner
Earl and Lesta Gipe — John and Edith Goulding — Holly Green
Wayne Guild — Vida Hamblet — Sue and Jerry Heister
Eileen Hills — Bill Hoffman and Jane Lawthers — Bruce Hoffman
Constance Hoffman and Chris Muller — Genevieve Hoffman
Arlene and Steve Jackson — Blake Jackson — Cammie Jackson
Joe and Margaret Jackson — Dick and Judy James
Genevieve Joncs — Phil and Arlene Judson
Walter and Anna Krehbiel — Erni and Joyce Laitinen
Betty Langdon — Frances Leach — Bonnie Lucier and Allen Ruble
Chester and Amy Luelling — Mac and Paula Mackinlay
Floyd and Helen Marchus — Elmore Martin — David Marvin
Marg McAstocker — Lowell and Janice McDaniel
Alice and Scott Messer — Mary Monahan — Audrey Neeley
Bertha Olin — Robert and Helen Overton — Jon and Carol Palley
Harriet and Ed Parsons — Bob and Shirley Peebles
Jimmie and Gretha Pelton — Robin and Daryl Peterson
Pat Rosier — Elizabeth and Arthur Salt
Harold and Gwen Schweitzer — Arden and Connie Sheets
Beth and Ward Sheller — Craig and Kathy Shinn — Lark Pelling
Erin Shinn — Caitlin Shinn — Ruth Smith
William and Iris Stevens — Earl and Marilyn Stoller

Graeme and Caroline Strickland — Linda and Bob Tackett
Joe Tackett — Marian and Elton Weber
William and Myra Weston — Art and Elsie Wilson
Donald and Maxine York — Robert and Marie York
Carol Zachary — Al and Nori Zieg — Roy and Betty Zimmer

Janie will live through her poetry and the memories shared
by all who knew or crossed paths with this remarkable
woman. Her own words best express the gratitude and love
she had for her family and friends.

Friends

I know that I must have God in my heart
If I would be all He means for me to be
But other aids, I know, will play a part.

When I remember what my friends have done
To help me on my way
I am most thankful, Lord, to you.

So little have I done alone;
Or, maybe, never would have done at all,
But for the love my friends have had for me
And their deep faith in what I sought to do.
I am most thankful, Lord to them and You.

— Janie Luelling Byrnes